UNDER
DOGS

UNDER DOGS

Man's Best Friend from
a whole new angle

Colin Crowdey

First published in Great Britain in 2020 by Trapeze
an imprint of The Orion Publishing Group Ltd
Carmelite House, 50 Victoria Embankment
London EC4Y 0DZ

An Hachette UK Company

1 3 5 7 9 10 8 6 4 2

A CIP catalogue record for this book is
available from the British Library.

ISBN (Hardback) 978 1 4091 9928 1
ISBN (eBook) 978 1 4091 9929 8

Printed in Italy

MIX
Paper from
responsible sources
FSC® C023419

www.orionbooks.co.uk

INTRODUCTION

Dogs. Man's best friend. They come in all shapes and sizes: big ones, little ones, hairy ones, spotty ones – the list goes on. We see pictures of dogs every day, and that is how I make my living – I'm a specialist dog photographer. But how often do we get to see them from underneath? If we're lucky we might get to tickle their tummy, but I wanted more. I wanted a different angle, which is why I started to take photos from below and my passion for 'underdogs' began – a truly unique and different perspective on a dog.

People thought I was crazy. 'You'll never get them to stand on glass,' they said. 'They'll jump off,' they said. Did they not appreciate what a dog would do for a piece of cheese or a sliver of ham?

As long as the dog was able to be lifted and wasn't too big or too heavy for the glass, they could be an underdog (I've turned down a Saint Bernard twice!!). I put out a call for willing volunteers and soon I had an array of dog owners wanting to see what it was all about.

This book is a collection of some of my favourite photographs. I hope you enjoy it.

(Note: No dogs were harmed during the making of this book!)

WINSTON, THE FRENCH BULLDOG

A three-year-old who would do anything for cheese!

DID YOU KNOW: *Don't let their smaller size fool you. The French Bulldog actually makes a good watchdog. They're highly intelligent and trainable, although training does require patience because they can be stubborn!*

OLLIE, THE COCKER SPANIEL

Ollie was nuts, not in a bad way, but nuts at 100 mph as lots of Cockers are! Ollie did something no dog has ever done before on the table: she rolled onto her back, scratched, then did the most perfect 360-degree roll off the table onto the floor, got up – slightly shocked – then jumped straight back on again! Crazy dog!

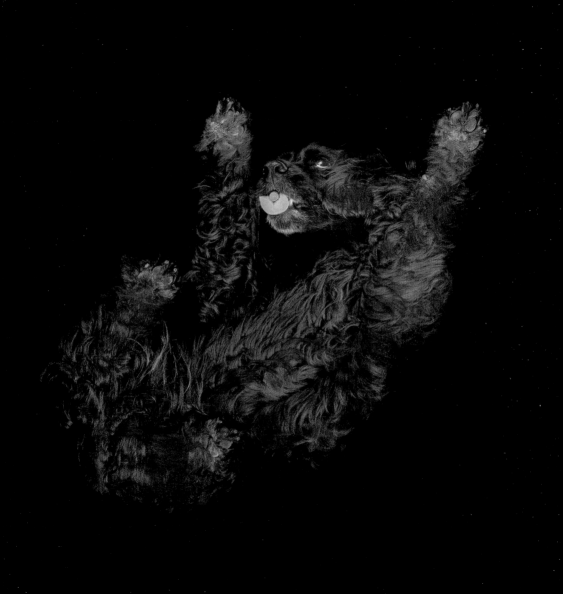

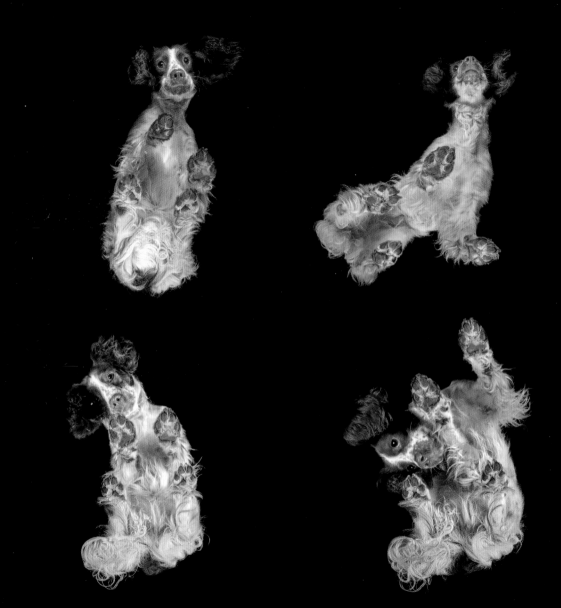

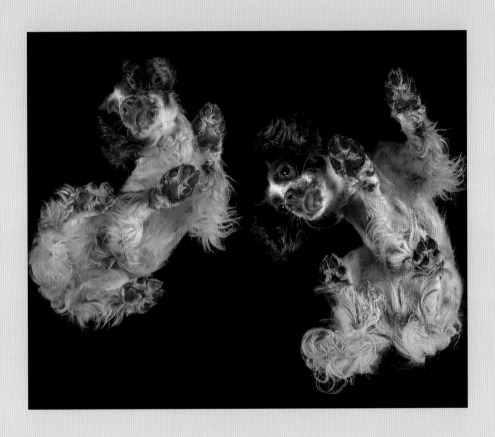

TONY, THE ITALIAN GREYHOUND

Tony is a ten-month-old who has a lot of personality packed into his tiny 5.5-kilogram body. He is an extremely cheeky boy with a cuteness overload, so you can never be cross with him. He has a short attention span but will entertain himself if necessary. Tony was a star and made his mum cry when he made a heart shape with his underdog body, which you can see on page 21!

DID YOU KNOW: *While Italian Greyhounds are known for their great speed, they would much rather relax than race. They can run faster than any other breed of dog, but would rather take a nap. It is their love of relaxation that has earned the Italian Greyhound the nickname, 'the forty-mile-per-hour couch potato'.*

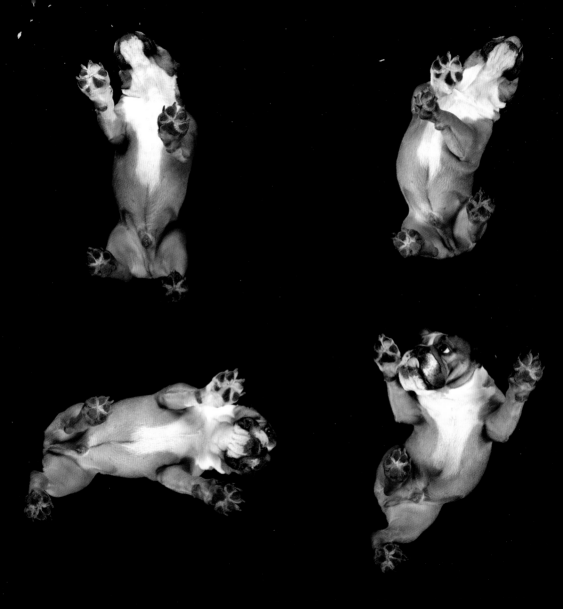

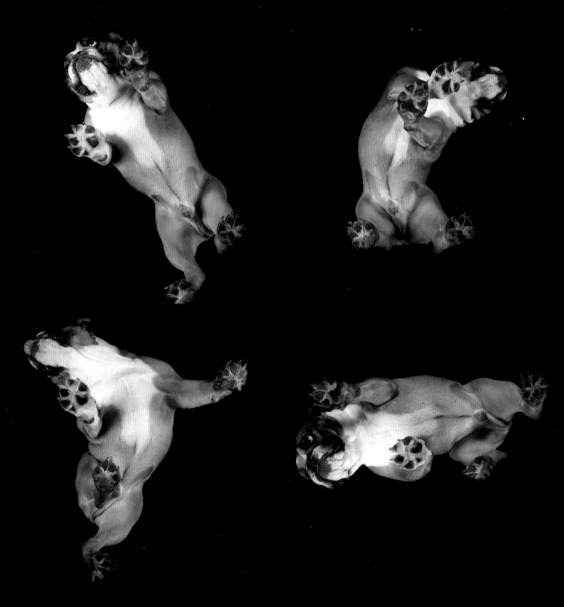

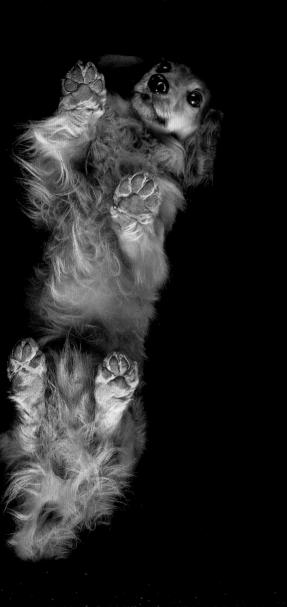

RIPPLE, THE LONG-HAIRED DACHSHUND

Ripple had the most amazing full-length coat and had recently showed at Crufts.

DID YOU KNOW: *The first Olympic mascot was a Dachshund. Waldi was born during the 1972 Munich Games' Organizing Committee's Christmas party in 1969.*

RODNEY, THE WHIPPET COLLIE CROSS

As a Whippet Collie Cross, his owner calls him a Whallie J. He looks like the Egyptian god Anubis – ridiculous ears, but he has a really big heart! Rodney didn't like the table much!

ZEPH, THE BORDER COLLIE

Zeph and Ziggy came to the studio as a pair – both were agility dogs, both with boundless energy. Three-year-old Zeph was (in his mum's opinion) going to be the super-confident one on the table, but surprisingly Zeph was very nervous to start with and needed to be coaxed and lavished with treats – he got there in the end.

ZIGGY, THE BORDER COLLIE

Seven years old – the 'old boy' of the pair – Ziggy got on the table straight away, posing left, posing right, looking down – and those paws!!!!

DID YOU KNOW: *A talented Border Collie named Striker holds the record for 'Fastest Car Window Opened by a Dog'. The canine rolled down the non-electric car window in 11.34 seconds.*

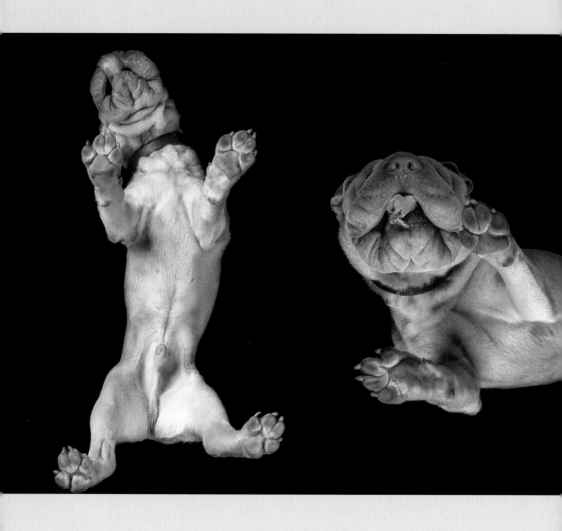

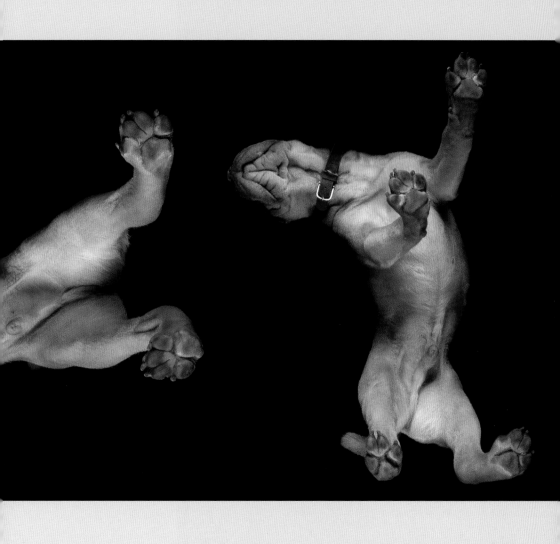

RUMOUR, THE MINIATURE AMERICAN SHEPHERD DOG

Mas Dogs (as they are affectionately known) are highly intelligent dogs, and Rumour was one of the most intelligent dogs to cross our table – he got it straight away, strutting his stuff and making all the right shapes and poses. Those eyes!!

DID YOU KNOW: *Often this breed of dog will have heterochromia – different-coloured eyes.*

RONNIE, THE BULLDOG

Rehomed when he was a puppy as his owners could not look after him, three-year-old Ronnie has been with his forever home family for two years and is such a confident and friendly dog – and looks super paw-some on the table!

DID YOU KNOW: *In 2015, Otto the skateboarding bulldog broke the Guinness World Record for 'Longest Human Tunnel Travelled Through by a Skateboarding Dog'. The talented canine soared under the legs of thirty people in Lima, Peru.*

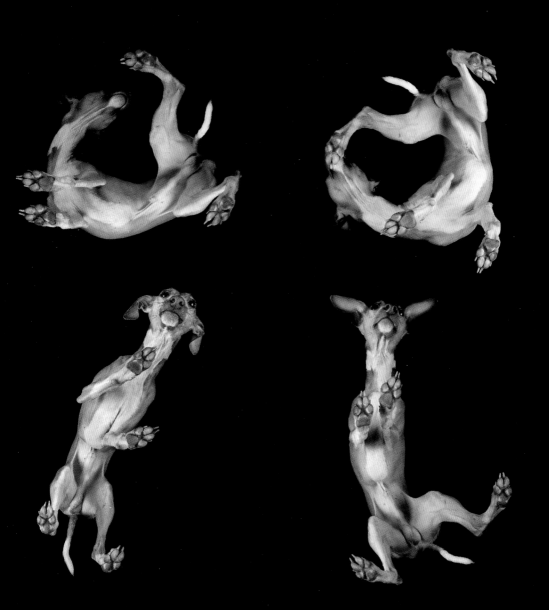

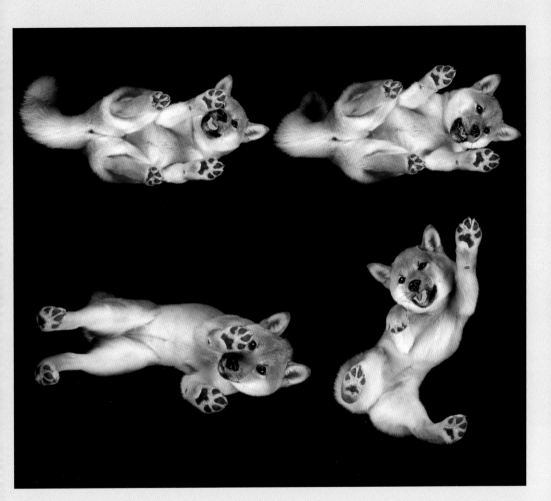

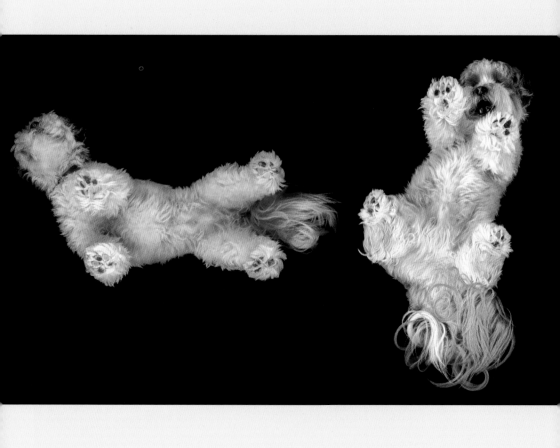

ALFIE, THE YORKSHIRE TERRIER

Alfie came in with his pal, Lisa, the Shihtzu. A young dog, he was a little scared of the glass table – but it helped when Lisa stood next to him.

DID YOU KNOW: *Yorkshire Terriers do not shed, so they depend on their owners to keep their fur in check. Left unattended, their coat will keep growing; in fact, it can grow to up to two feet long!*

MADDIE, THE LURCHER

Maddie was one of three Lurchers in the studio at the same time – Kiera and Dex the other two. Maddie was thirteen and a proper diva! But boy, did she rock the table – such a poser.

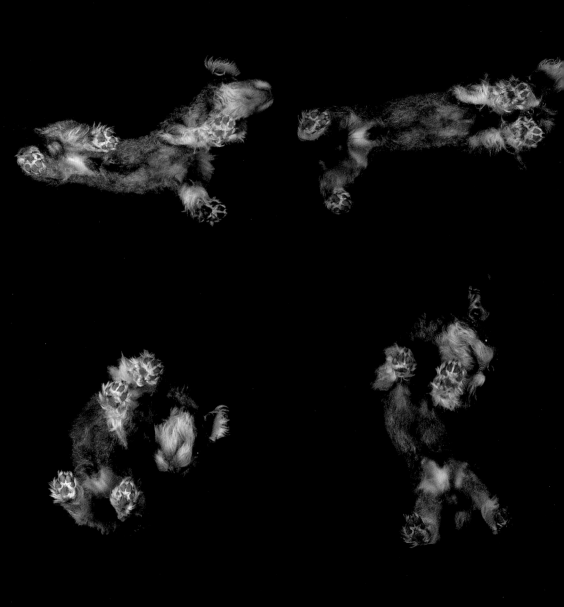

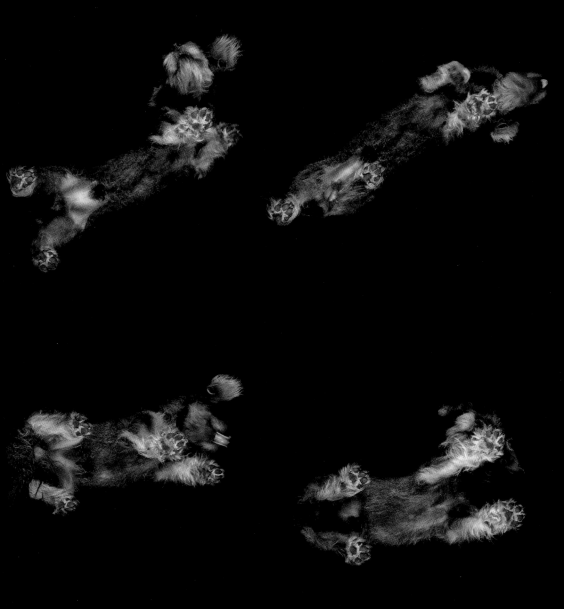

PURDY, THE FIELD SPANIEL

Purdy had the most amazing ears (and paws). She was a bit nervous on the table – being only one year old this was probably a very daunting experience for her.

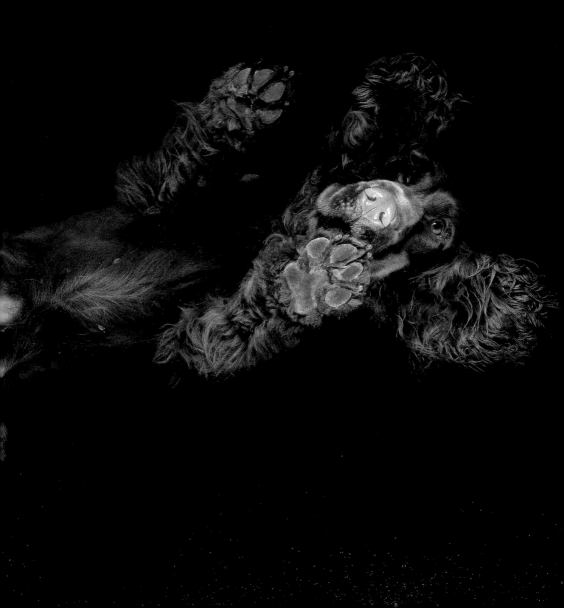

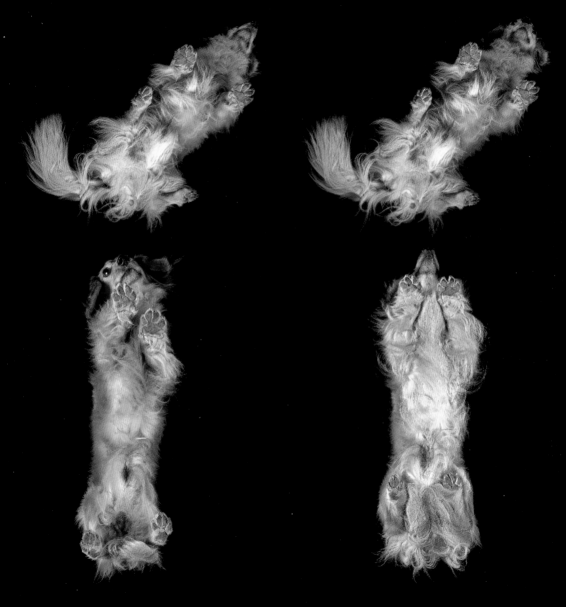

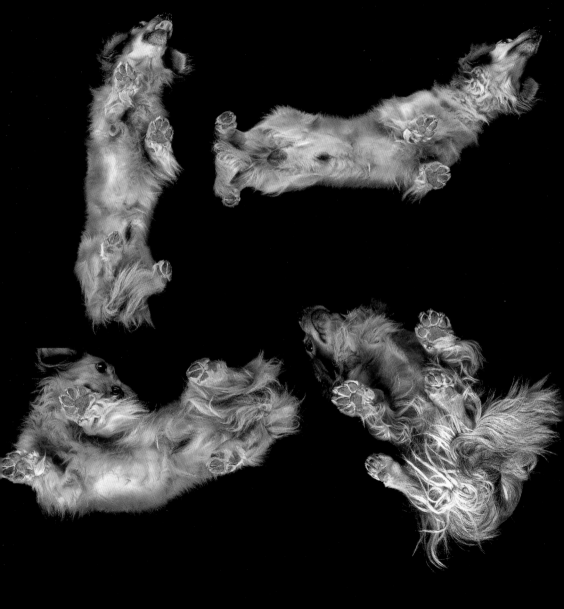

OLIVE, THE SPRINGER SPANIEL

An energetic eleven-month-old, Olive loves destroying anything she can. Also loves cuddles, chasing leaves, cats and anything that moves. She looked super-cool on the table.

DID YOU KNOW: *President George W. Bush had a spaniel called Spot – and President George H.W. Bush had one called Millie.*

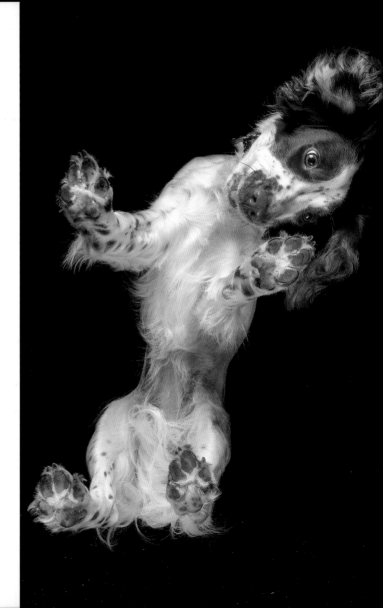

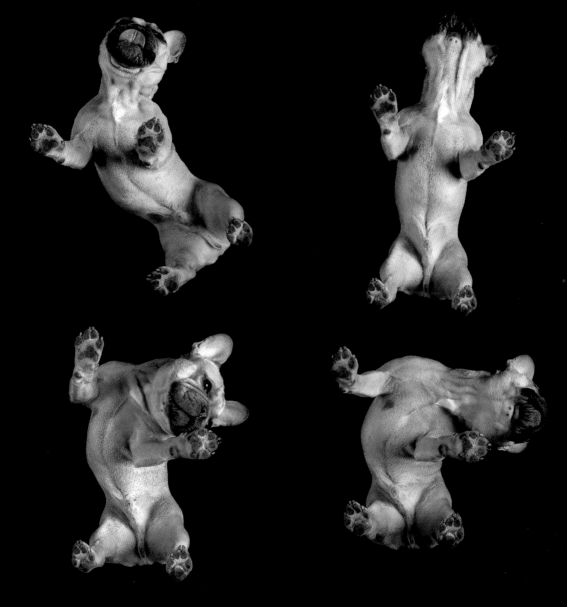

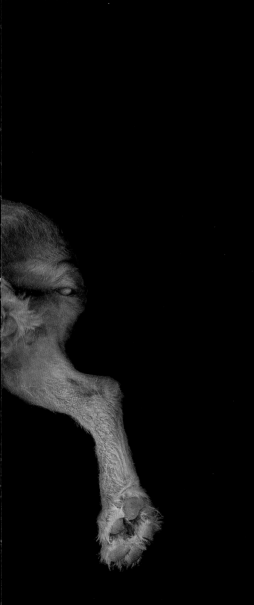

NELLIE, THE WIRE-HAIRED VIZSLA

Four years old, Nellie has spondylitis, which slows her down a little. Nellie loves life! On the day of her underdog shoot, we were in the midst of a biblical rainstorm; water and glass don't mix with the underdog table, and coupled with the fact Nelly was a long-legged dog, we had to be super-careful. Even after a good rubbing down with the towel and a blow-dry with our studio fur drier, she ended up doing the splayed leg crash on the table – it sounds quite funny but is scary for a dog! She needed plenty of calming and a watchful eye from her owner – but she took an amazing underdog photograph in the end.

DID YOU KNOW: *A Vizsla's top speed is 40 mph.*

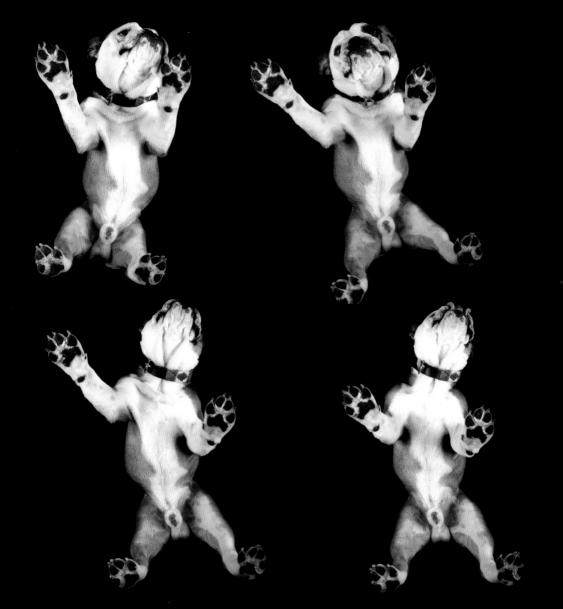

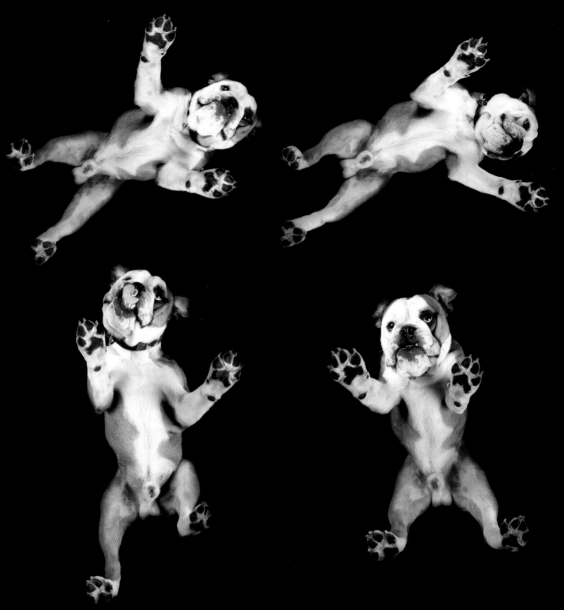

LUNA, THE BORDER COLLIE

Luna is another Christmas dog, this time a Christmas Day puppy – she's now six years old. Luna was abandoned by her mother at two weeks old and was rescued from her owner three weeks later as she was no longer wanted. She now has an amazing life with her forever home parents.

MATTIE, THE SHAR PEI

A ten-month-old apricot with blue-beige eyes – what a stunning dog! Mattie loves to chase squirrels and could perform about fifteen tricks – but only where a treat was involved! Mattie struggled with the table as he is a big dog!

DID YOU KNOW: *From the late 1960s to the mid-1970s, the Shar Pei was listed by Guinness World Records as the rarest dog breed in the world.*

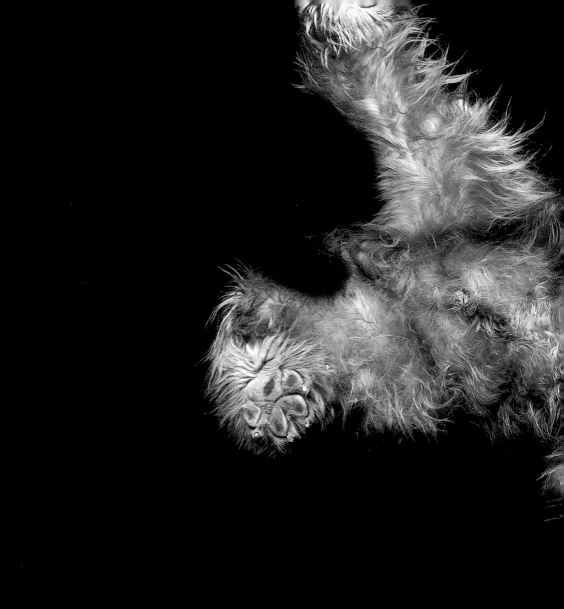

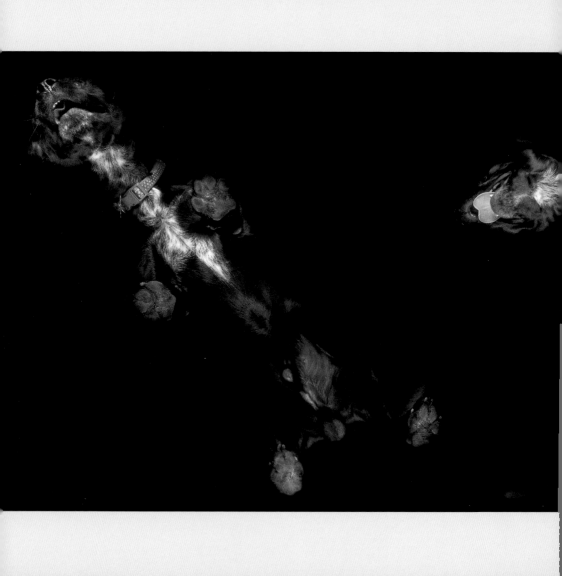

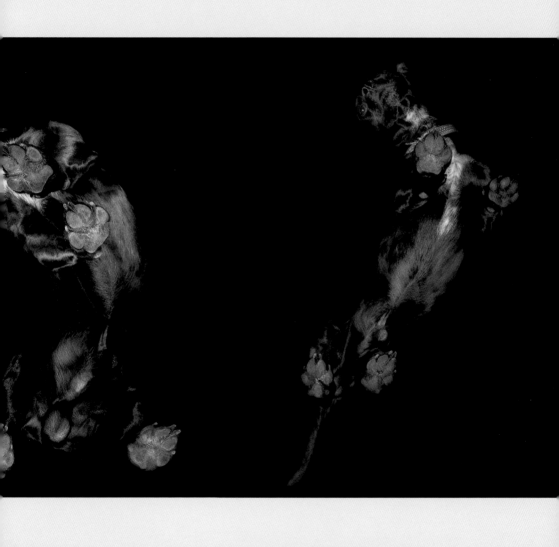

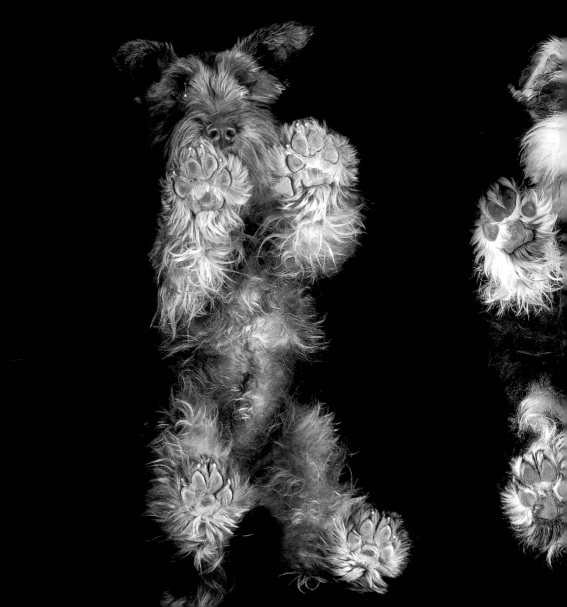

MAX AND MOLLY, THE MINIATURE SCHNAUZERS

Fourteen weeks old, Max was the confident one and posed like a natural. Eleven-week-old Molly was more nervous but came into her own when we had Max on the table with her!

DID YOU KNOW: *Miniature Schnauzers were farm dogs that were used as ratters, bred to hunt and kill any uninvited guests. The thick facial hair was sometimes matted down into a dense armour that protected the canine's face from any potential retaliation from its prey.*

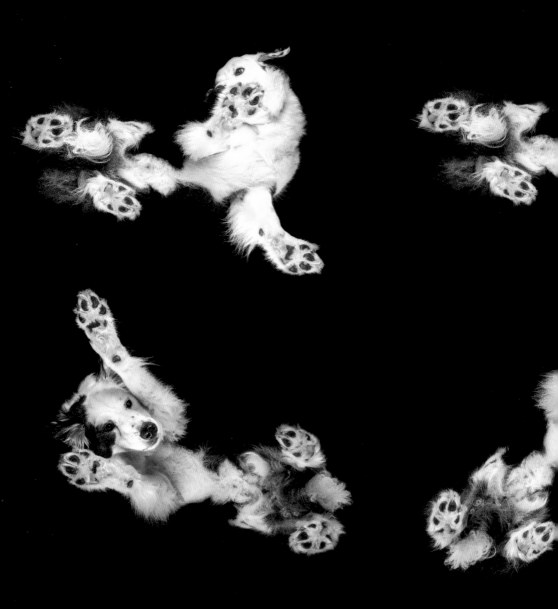

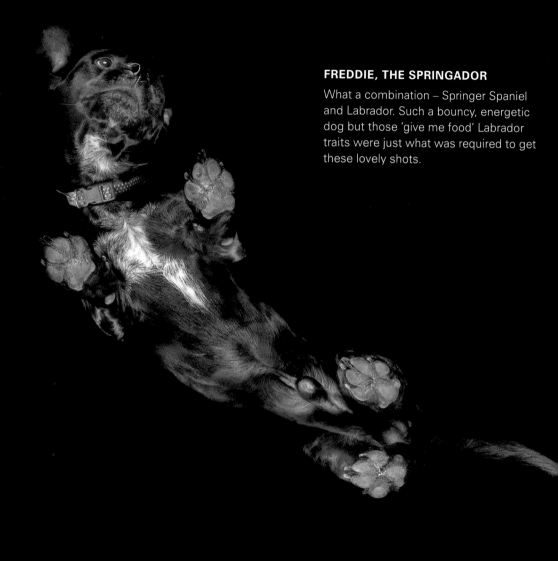

FREDDIE, THE SPRINGADOR

What a combination – Springer Spaniel and Labrador. Such a bouncy, energetic dog but those 'give me food' Labrador traits were just what was required to get these lovely shots.

DAVE, THE ENGLISH BULLDOG

Ten months old, Dave was such a character – stubborn, funny and lazy! He was more than happy on the glass and just look at that tongue! He might look a little bit grumpy, but he was a great big softy.

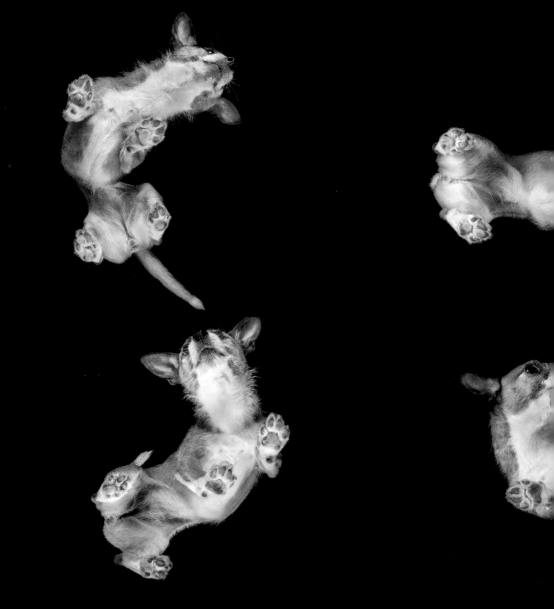

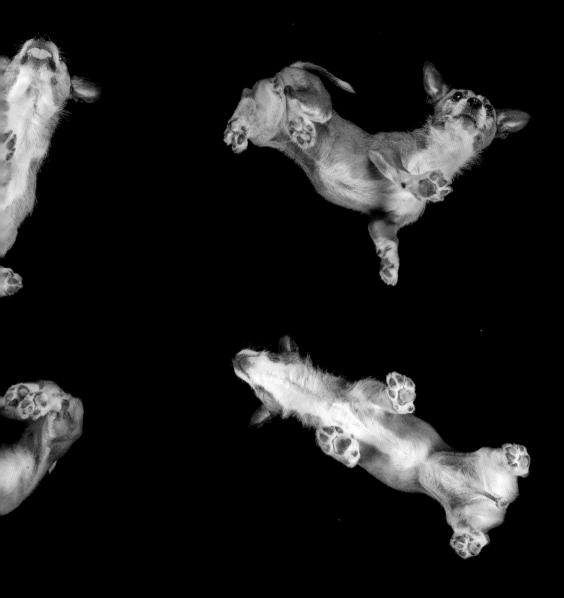

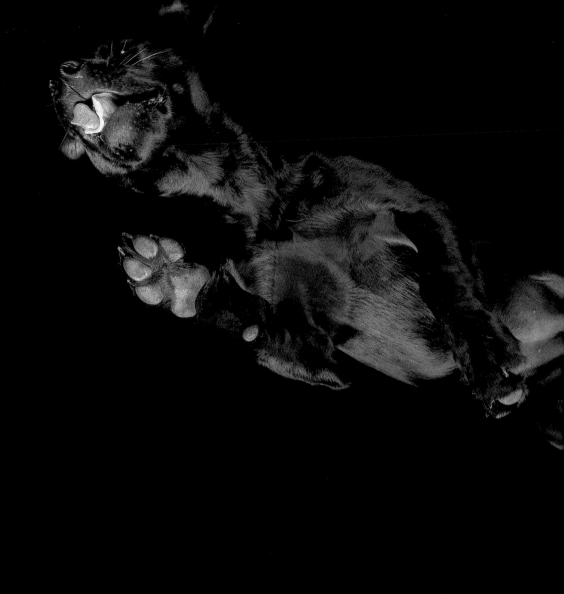

IVY, THE LABRADOODLE

Born on Christmas Eve, Ivy was only twelve weeks old when she graced the underdog table. She was fearless and super laid-back, and Mum told us her life revolved around jumping and gravy bones!

JIMMY, THE WIRE-HAIRED DACHSHUND

We've had a few sausage dogs grace the underdog table and Jimmy was one of my favourites. He loved it; he was a natural underdog.

DID YOU KNOW: *Unlike other Dachshunds, the Wire-Haired Dachshund is known for being friendly and outgoing with new people.*

INCA, THE SHIBA INU

Is it a fox, is it a cuddly toy? No, it's the loveliest Japanese Shiba Inu you could ever meet. The fluffiest tail and the cutest face! Only four months old, Inca was such a natural on the table. She has the longest walks in the entire world because her owners are stopped by EVERYONE they meet out walking!!

DID YOU KNOW: *In 2004, an earthquake struck the village of Yamakoshi, in Japan. When her family's home collapsed, a Shiba Inu named Mari sprang into action to save her puppies and her elderly owner. She moved her puppies to a safe place and then found and woke up her owner, who had been trapped under a fallen cabinet. He managed to free himself and was evacuated from the area by helicopter. He was forced to leave Mari and her pups behind, but when he returned two weeks later, he found them all alive.*

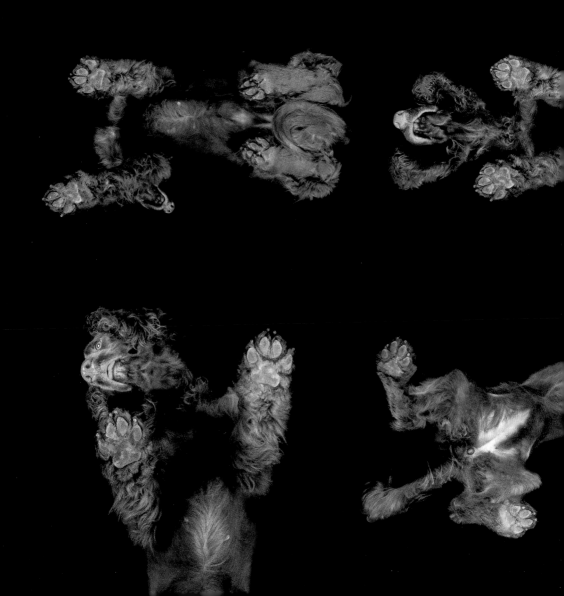

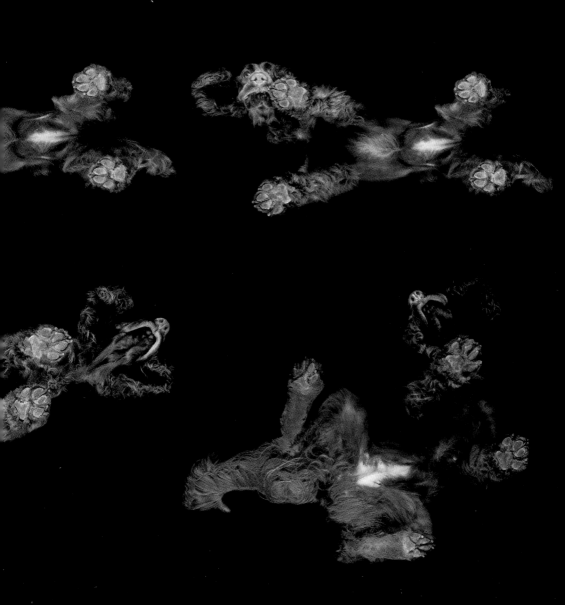

BEN, THE COLLIE

Sadly, Ben was none too
impressed with the table.
In fact, he got on it, laid
down, and that was where
stayed!!

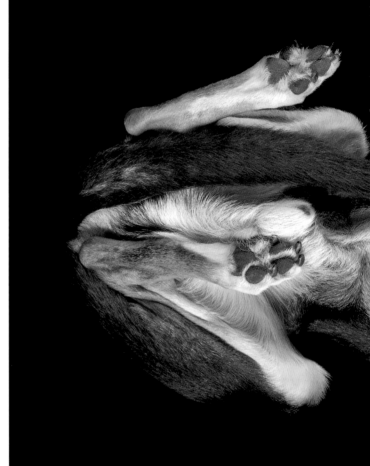

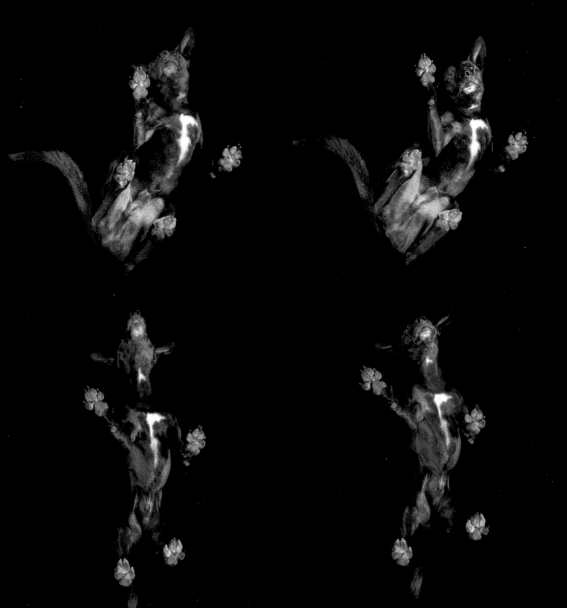

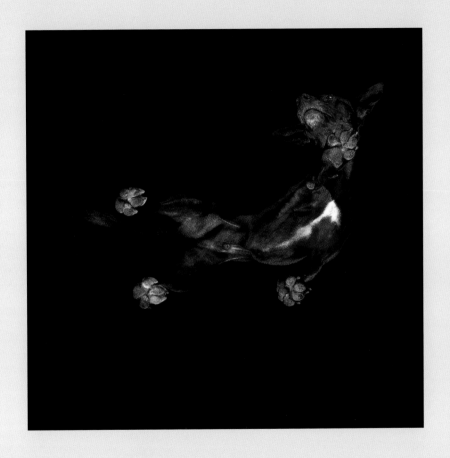

ALI, THE DALMATIAN – AKA ALI THE DALI

There are only two rules in the studio: firstly, safety is paramount and secondly, an underdog only gets two chances on the table! But Ali, the twelve-week-old liver-spotted Dalmatian, well, she broke the rules big time! Three times she was on the table, three times she was petrified, but three times Mum convinced me to try again, and on the fourth attempt she got it (Ali, not the mum), and she rocked the glass table!

DID YOU KNOW: *Dalmatian puppies are born snow-white. Pups generally don't develop their trademark spots until about four weeks of age.*

BUDDY, THE LABRADOODLE

Buddy was just five months old when he came for his underdog shoot but wasn't at all nervous, with puppy enthusiasm in abundance! Although Buddy had to be rehomed when he was only twelve weeks old because his owners were unable to look after him, he now has his new forever home and is absolutely living puppy life to the full – even getting the 'underdog' experience too!

DID YOU KNOW: *Not only can Labradoodles track their owner's location, but when they are lost, they have the ability to find their way back home.*

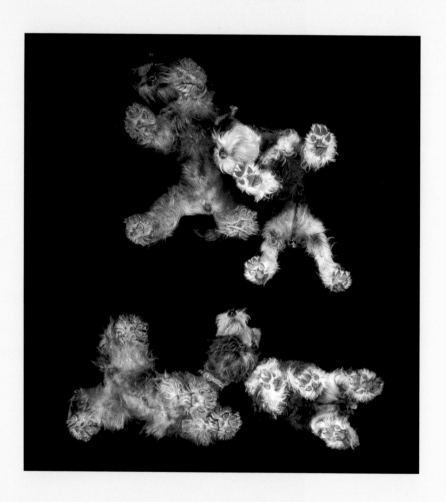

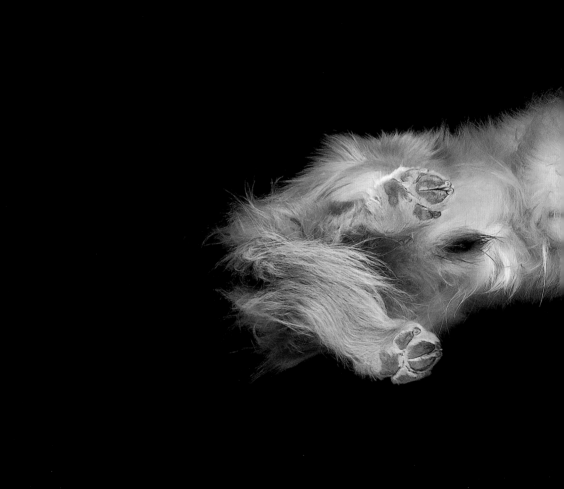

BORIS, THE TIBETAN TERRIER CROSS

My first-ever underdog. Boris didn't have the best start in life – he was found abandoned in a Tesco car park, curled up in a fluffy ball in a supermarket trolley. He was quickly rehomed and is a great family pet, as well as being my original underdog.

Boris took to the glass table instantly and was not fazed by anything. Look at those paws and that tail!

DID YOU KNOW: *The Tibetan Terrier came from a region of Tibet known as the Lost Valley, so-named because an earthquake destroyed the major road that allowed access to the valley in the fourteenth century. The Tibetan Terrier has existed for at least two thousand years.*

ARCHIE, THE BORDER COLLIE

A thirteen-week-old Border Collie full of life and mischief who adores his older 'brother', seven-year-old Ben (who's far from convinced!).

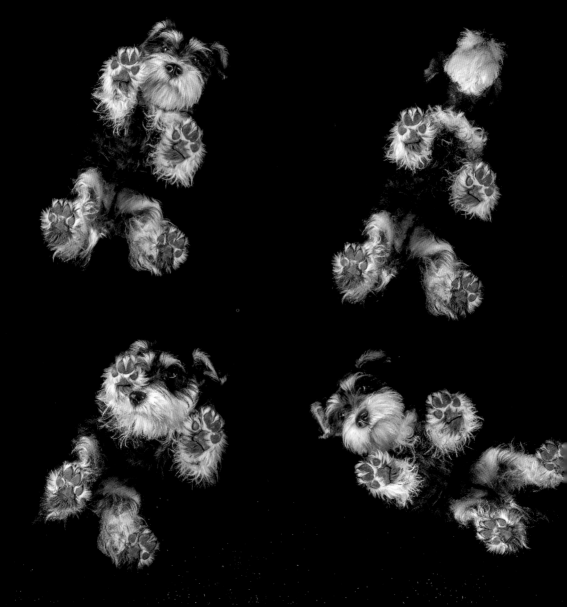

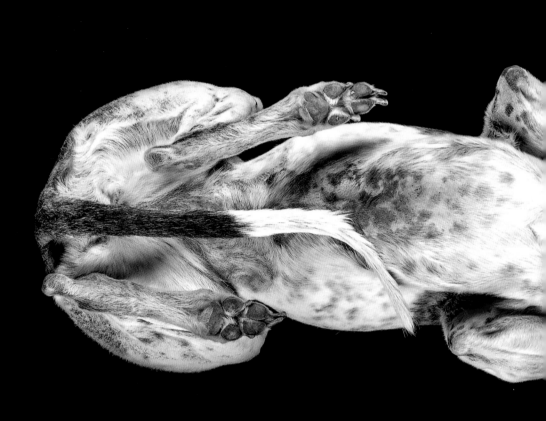

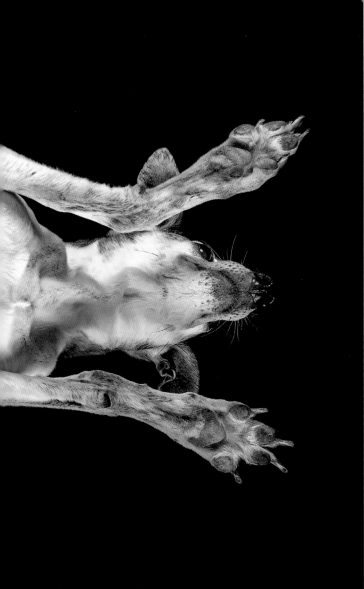

KIERA, THE LURCHER

Of the three Lurchers
we were photographing,
Kiera, aged ten, was the
most difficult to work with
– she was very shy and
timid, and lying down was
pretty much all she could
manage.

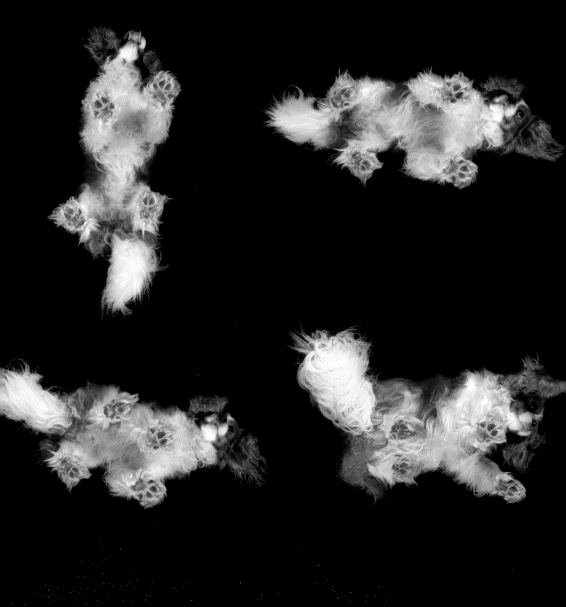

LISA, THE SHIH TZU

An adorable Shih Tzu with the fiercest haircut! Lisa is totally blind and selectively deaf so it was pretty easy to manoeuvre her on the table. She was there with her buddy Alfie, the Yorkshire Terrier.

DID YOU KNOW: *The Mandarin phrase 'Shih Tzu' translates to 'little lion'. The Shihtzu was likely given this name because of its association with the Tibetan Buddhist God of Learning, who, according to legend, travelled with a small lion dog that could transform into a full-sized lion.*

DEX, THE LURCHER

Dex was one of the longer dogs who graced my
glass table. Aged nine, he was a rescue dog bred
purely for hunting – although now retired!

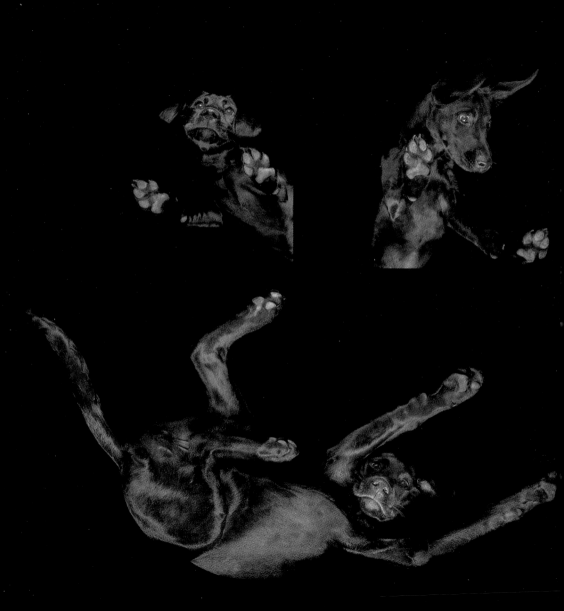

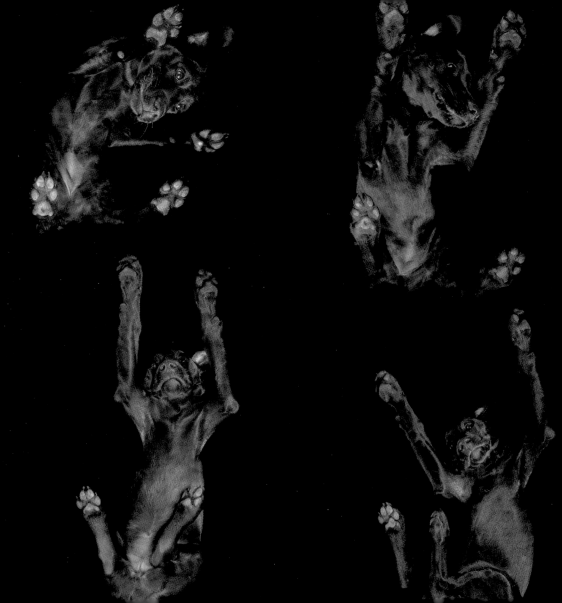

FINN, THE COCKERPOO

Lovely Finn took a while
to get his underdog 'feet'
but oh, such a sweet dog!

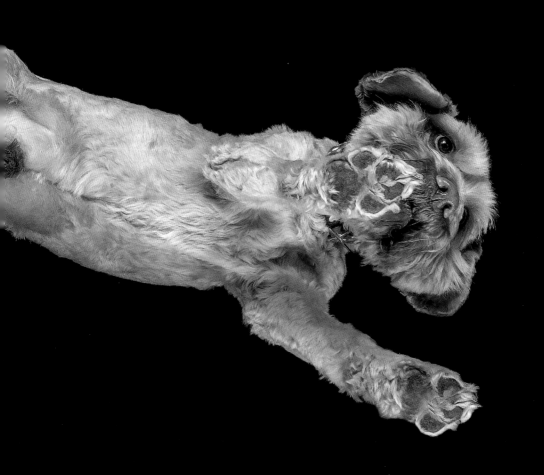

DORA, THE SPRINGER SPANIEL

We love spaniels in the studio, but Dora was no ordinary spaniel – Dora is famous! She has been in a number of TV films and commercials and was the perfect dog for the table: look left Dora, look right Dora, twist a shape Dora – nothing was too difficult for this spaniel.

JINTY, THE JACK RUSSELL CROSS

Jinty is no stranger to the camera. She can be seen on many a TV advert – she really is a star! Being an underdog was all in a day's work for such a seasoned media dog!

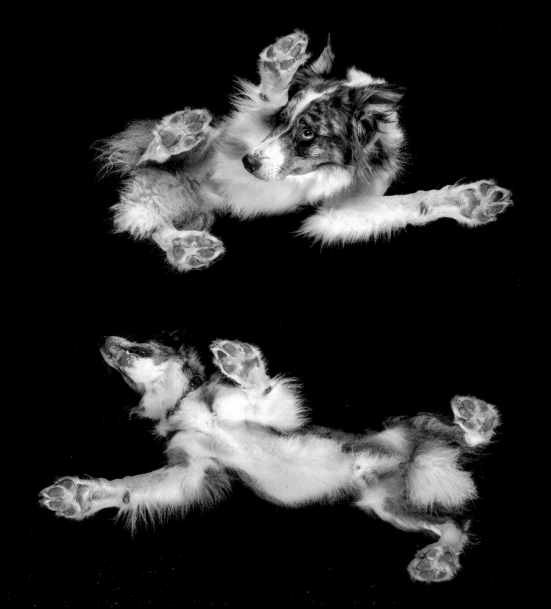

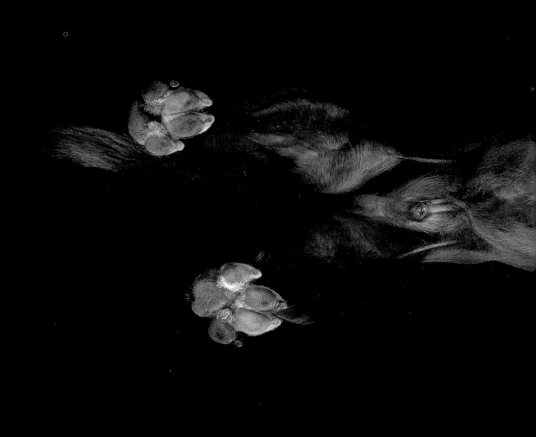

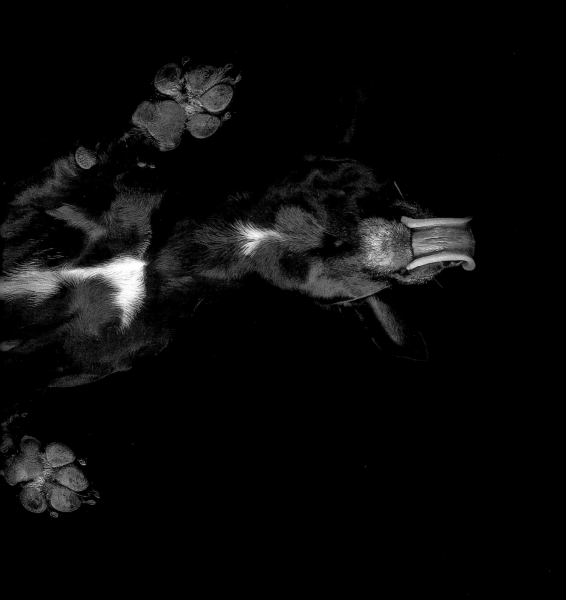

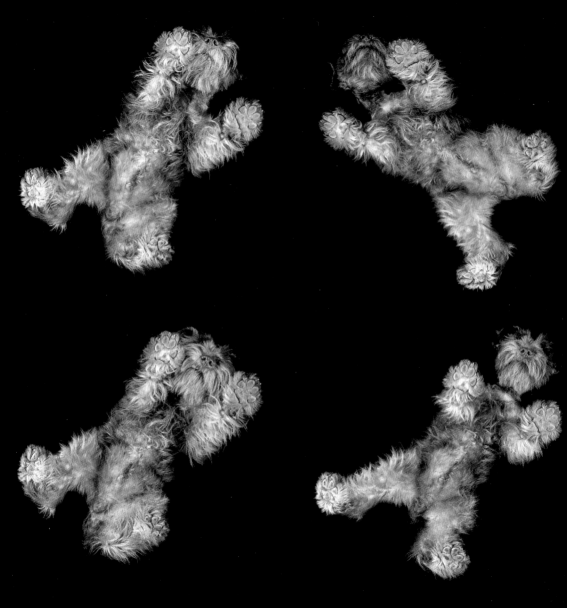

GERTIE, THE SPRINGER SPANIEL

Aged three, Gertie was rather shy, but look at her wonderful markings and gorgeous paws.

DONNIE, THE AMERICAN BULLDOG/ENGLISH SPRINGER SPANIEL CROSS

A natural poser in front of the camera and a real cheeky chap whose tail never stopped wagging, Donnie was still very much a puppy at heart. He was one of the largest breeds we've had on the table, and has the most amazing paws. As you'll see that's a running theme where an underdog is concerned – it's all about the paws!

Oh, and Donnie likes cats!!

DID YOU KNOW: *Despite being short-haired, American Bulldogs are heavy shedders.*

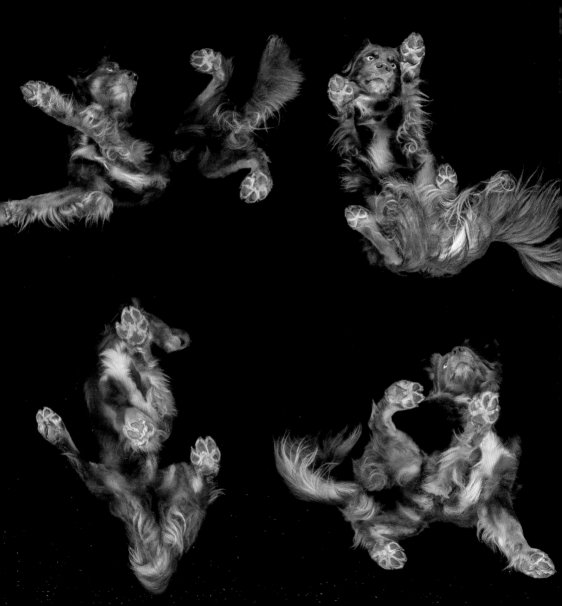

HONEY, THE CAVALIER KING CHARLES SPANIEL

Sadly, Honey is a three-year-old rescue dog who is completely deaf – probably a good thing she couldn't hear her owner's choice words when she wouldn't pose on the table!! But our trusty treats shone through and we soon got her nose working overtime for the treats and she rocked the table!

DID YOU KNOW: *An urban legend claims that Charles II issued a special decree granting King Charles Spaniels permission to enter any establishment in the UK, overriding the 'no dog except guide dogs' rule.*

CASSIE, THE JACK RUSSELL TERRIER

Definitely one of those dogs who'll do anything for a snack! She wolfed down all my doggy treats, but oh, what a poser she was!

DID YOU KNOW: *Jack Russell Terriers are incredibly smart and have a strong drive to explore the world around them. This means that not only can they excel at various training exercises but also that they have to be intellectually and physically stimulated all day long.*

These aren't dogs that will sit quietly in the corner and ponder the finer intricacies of squirrel chasing – they are dogs that will tirelessly seek out the squirrel, find it and give it a run for its acorns!

LEO, THE COLLIE

A red merle collie, Leo has the most stunning features and is one of the friendliest dogs I've ever had in the studio – and that's without tempting him with our famed gravy bones! Leo rocked the table like a natural, did everything we asked of him and more. Leo can come back any time!

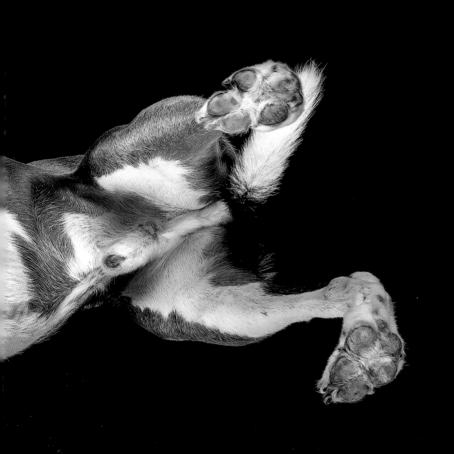